at the barre

at the barre

poems by

candyce clayton

Introduction by Jenné Andrews

HOLY COW! Press · MINNEAPOLIS · 1978

Grateful acknowledgement is made to the following publications in which some of these poems first appeared: *A Coloring Book of Poetry for Adults* (Vanilla Press), *Minnesota Poetry Outloud*, *Moons and Lion Tailes*, *North Country Anvil*, *Oxygen*, and *Twin Cities Women Poets Valentine's Day Anthology* (Smith Park Press).

Copyright © 1978 by Candyce Clayton

ISBN 0-930100-00-X

Library of Congress Number: 77-89854

Cover photograph of The Classical Ballet Academy of Minnesota (St. Paul, Minnesota) and photograph of Candyce and Croix by Edward Bock.

Special thanks to Jenné Andrews for her generous editorial attention to these poems.

First Printing

All rights reserved. No part of this book may be reproduced or transmitted in any form without permission from the publisher.

Printed in the USA

Publisher's address:

HOLY COW! Press
P.O. Box 618
Minneapolis, Minnesota 55440

Principal Distributor:

TRUCK DISTRIBUTION SERVICE
1645 Portland Avenue
St. Paul, Minnesota 55104

for my grandmothers

*eleanora josephine kirchoff clayton
mae mary evans larned*

for my friend

sally bayless richards

for my child

croix cambria clayton

sell everything. but save the dance for yourself.

CONTENTS

To Make One's Life A Dance

    Introduction by Jenné Andrews   ix

I. *at the barre*

    snow song for my apple son   4
    the man's hands   6
    killing frost   7
    north dakota grandparents   9
    winter storm : minnesota, 1975   10
    the coming and going of ivory   11
    wild grass   14
    the last time i saw richard   15
    oh the mirror   16
    stalking pisces   18
    harbor   21
    at the barre   22

II. *the dance*

    washing garden greens   26
    the plain therapy of new england   28
    the alliance of new sisters   30
    naming the parts we keep   31
    letter from denmark   34
    the ballet   35
    piano lessons   36
    the emperor's new teeth   37
    putting up against winter   38
    waitress poem   40
    passage   42
    famine of woman   44
    nightwatch   46
    song for the womb fruit   47

the study of the dance has at its core the discipline of the barre. the barre is wooden, affixed to the studio wall at hip height.

it is at the barre where all movement begins. through the repetition of strenuous physical exercise and taut concentration, the components of grace slowly come into relief. as one posture or phrase of the dance achieves definition, another, alongside it, appears vague. the dancer returns again and again to the barre to construct character into what was vague, to transfuse a statement of the body with a sense of endurance and gift of insight.

the impossible war between body and image is relentless, and we are forever at the barre.

I

at the barre

it is at the barre where all movement begins

snow song for my apple son

it's going to blizzard
but you don't know what snow is.
you sit with your gown high
fat apple knees exposed
like an orchard's best fruit
in its best summer season.
the snow holds us like an envelope
and i write a letter on white paper
to a friend so far south
that even when children grow up
they don't know what snow is.
last night i heard the snow coming.
do you remember?
i said *'listen,*
that deft-footed silence
is the sound of approach.'
the sky groaned like a tent.
near the west a great rent
and we stood beneath the yawning seam
our feet in rubbers
prepared to love the stuff like a gift,
your eyes as blue as the sky beyond apple boughs.
this morning we see someone has turned
this toy city upside down.
for a while
everywhere
the snow.
we are lucky ones to be in the dawn.
we are dreamers, we are a marriage party
the avenue our white veil train.
we hum gershwin and cruise like smooth jazz
past the governor's mansion
with as much snow to shovel as any
commoner's dwelling.

we sing out *'bess, you is my woman now'*
and blue light suits us.
and tonight
when we're snow tired and sung-out
we'll draw apples, color them red,
smelling summer in our paper.

the man's hands

you come to me in the
cold night
wrapped in folds
of the rain skirt.
not you, actually,
but your hands.
ghosts of your hands.
the fires you built through one
brittle north winter
working the wood into flame.
the cold hands, skin split and dry
smelling of bark and ashes
as you'd touch me.
brushing your daughter's hair
the same way you'd prepare vegetables
or fix the truck.
the same way of putting breath
into anything you'd hold.

i have not seen you in months.
we will not face this winter together.
but in tonight's rain
(they say it will turn to snow)
the last of the leaves are taken
and softly, through the wet streets
lift like ghosts,
brushing high windows
with a breath of bark and ashes.

killing frost

between the election news
and the weather report
(it's going to freeze tonight)
the broadcaster tells your story
in ten seconds.
you, a ward of the state hospital,
"mentally incompetent and mute"
wandered from the picnic yesterday
are lost in a vermont state park while police
and other employees of the state search.
they will have to seek out historic landmarks,
the red berries of mountain ash,
muskrat and pinecones
to find you, mikey.
they say you
*"do not have the mental capacity
to make judgements in your own defense,"*
that you do not speak, but recognize
your name.
and who frightened the tongue out of you?
and who gave you cause
to defend yourself
then found you weak and silent?
what was it you heard in the pulse of autumn
that sent you from your keepers,
what dance burst in your heels
that sent you deeper into the woods,
what shiny object glinted
in the trees ahead?

out in the garden the damp breath of dusk
sits heavy.
death hides in the cold blue wind.
tonight a killing frost.
i survey the vegetable patch
the dumb victims.
i pick every tomato i can find.
they are all green.
they are all green and small and no good
for eating
but i can't will them to the night.
no sacrifice of mine will prevent winter.
close to the ground, at the bottom
of the vine
i find my prize, a single rosy fruit
weighted in its ripeness
its skin holds the last sunset.

hang low on your vine, mikey.
wear your wanderlust like a brilliant cloak
and let the indian summer song
which breathed so warm in the shell of your ear
be the lullabye you could never request.
deep into the silver house of night
your body kindles in its new language
a naming to voyage from hunger
a canopy of frost over those who seek you out
a chant
that this is a country built on survival
of the fittest.
that the greatest killing frost is found
not in autumn forests
but in federal corridors
and that the state has never been
a gentle mother
gathering her helpless ones
in from the dark.

north dakota grandparents

he was an older man,
had tough eyes, hard lines
in his face.
sixty-nine north dakota snows
had frozen that face
that many seasons of sandstorms
ground down his throat.
he'd strut around the fields
around the barnyard
a haughty cock
cursing and chuckling.
said it was his wife
who was most nearly crazy
though they never got too close
to him, either.
he'd pound his fists on her
grandmother's lace.
the jelly goblets would shake.
she'd just bow down her head
as though her nails were important.
nails were important to her.
christ hung on the east bedroom wall
and at night
while the old man would strut around
the barnyard
kick manure in the face of the moon,
she'd fold her swollen fingers
round those rosary beads
and the tears would flow,
and he'd come in
from the north dakota dark
and wouldn't even try
to warm
her side of the bed.

winter storm: minnesota, 1975

now the winter's here.
snowplows rumble past in the night,
orange workers of the state
cleaving drifts from my house
to yours.
no one sets out.
along the avenue frame houses
bear the dark blizzard.
pieces of yellow light
patch snow beneath kitchen windows.
someone moves there
setting water to boil, drawing the shade.
late night news tells of
the tying off of country from town
stranded cars and cattle,
kerosene running low.
nearly out of sugar,
and the wood still damp.

my half-known friend, i see you
after the unlighting
of the last lamp
you, wrapped in lap-robe
working in the room facing the lake,
fingers smudged with pastel,
your small house so deep
in snow.
our rooms grow cold
as the ancient winter sky reaches high
into the throat of night.
the blizzard moves out across the lake
toward the prairie.

the coming and going of ivory

1.

the cold has never had such a stink
to it before.
jungles of ice overrun the cherry and
willow bough.
cold broad as the backs of elephants
rides every window
cold sharper than the newest angry tusk
breaks through
but no glass shatters, no ivory appears.

2.

the winter's tune is not pianissimo.
no denouement relieves us.
the icescape looms
etching the lungs, other cavities.
we wonder how long it will take
this slow mutiny of the flesh.
there are not comforters enough
and the tea with its quiet heat
that sends us to sleep four in a bed,
frost on the floor
traces to the warm places of dreams.

3.

i can't tell whose dream i'm having.
is it my son's
who measures the world in female voices,
who pushes his baby face
into my flannel shoulder, mouthing
for a nipple, in sleep
perhaps hunting seals
his man's body wrapped in skins.

he calls to the seals in their own voice.
but they do not come. they flee.
he has told them to flee
in their own voice he has said
'hasten, my seals, hasten,
for the man in me and the woman
in me, we make love to you
with our need, our great human need
for the bodies of lesser animals.
hasten, hasten.'

   4.

ah, but for one.
and in this dream the little one
with whiskers like a french fan
advances to my man-dressed son
drawn by the harpoon.
in the seal's eyes it is a stave,
the man-child a shepard of
shared language.
the small seal rolls onto its side
its tough hide oiled
in message.
with his fingertips, my son deciphers.
the little seal is going blind.
he reads faster.
the seal's song is a passage of ivory.
the last strange words begin to fade
to recede.

far out at sea an island of seals
is turning to the east.

5.

my son with his breath of milk
has burrowed between my breasts
and someone else is having my dream.
in the alley beneath the bedroom window
snow has piled so thick
it has become a shelter.
it is the north wing
of my house
and i have gone to the root cellar
for potatoes, winter potatoes
to boil a pot of tubers
to set for a winter supper
while we listen for a thaw in the wind,
playing over the cherry grove
soft as felted ivories.

wild grass

what do i say
to a man
with wild grass
where the heart grows.

what do i say to you
having lain in a wedding bed,
while i've never stayed
past an afternoon
with any one man.

what do i say
when i never see your eyes.
when your voice changes
every day
like wind over wild grass.

the last time i saw richard
   [*"...all romantics meet the same fate some day"*]
                              —joni mitchell

waiting for the phone to ring
wading through september
smell the sweet apples, their ripe odor
musking up the leaf-fall air.
through september, sky a deep lake
drastic blue
and placid. placid
like the quiet fever of expect.
the soft lurching dance
of something brilliant dying.

late afternoon sun finds
the autumn carnival of leaves,
performers balanced beneath the spotlight
their costumes shine transparent
through their veins, their lives.
stunts are what they eat.
that last death-defying leaf
caught dizzy in the drastic blue.
caught for a flight-second
in some pocket of september.
poised
over the silent telephone wires.

oh the mirror

reaching at you
watching slow the rounding ways
you quickly go.
good day you pray
you practise
hid inside the guide
you never bid.
oh i was clever
i saw lean and long the glance
you took to town, the dance
behind that soft sad smile
that lay back sleeping
all the while
clutching sly to frown.
the face the face and
oh the mirror
turning brightly flashes nearer.
skip the handhold
press those eyes between a thigh
a sky of sighs.
but look
look
how apple shiny squeaks so red
like hollow cheeks that draw
from dusty manuscripts
of staffs and chords and sung off-beats.
you beat me
when i tried to say
i saw you young.

you got there first
and i was wicked
i was thirst, a water sign
don't work with earth,
or fire, or air.
it's fair to reach
if on the way
the prayer is beached
and busts the day.

stalking pisces

stalking pisces, riverfriend
in mid december
what sure end must surely come
must bend the bones like muskrat traps
caught tight in weaving seaweed.
the woods filled up
all winter long
with lovely words, with snow's soft song
and all the pine trees
in the fields, the smoke-late skies
that watched us,
lingered there for one last dream
another phrase
to dance the log fire
secret, hot,
impress us with
we've got or not.

a tallish man with porcelain skin
and hands to rock a woman well,
empties wine jugs, gently rolls
the homemade quilt down
off your shelf
then loves you
through his curlblack hair, his back
a lumberjack.
and while you're sleeping
moon rides high,
calls him down the icy bank.
he glides past like riverfolk
crouching in cold sleep.
then reaching for the man's sweet mouth
the pillow's pulled.

TO MAKE ONE'S LIFE A DANCE

Candyce Clayton's poems are written with acuity and tenderness. They are like songs in the way they move, and in their movement toward and away from an essential perception, a thematic or primary image, they are indeed like the dance. By their confluence of imagery, gathering of associations, the poems bring experience and meaning gradually into "relief".

These poems also speak to an integrate life. One strives—and in the best poetry written in our American idiom, this seems to be our work—to mediate worlds within worlds without and within; to allow opposing worlds to exist in a symmetry, a form, a specific and burnished language.

In the poem "the coming and going of ivory" the recurrence of snow becomes a migration of beasts with tusks of ice. Later in the poem, in a dream, a seal speaks to the poet's infant son about something lost; that which is white, valuable, pure and ephemeral: "the seal's song is a passage of ivory."

This poem is a marvelous parable of psychic journey; the journey between consciousness and sleep, how we travel in dreams to the edge of an ice flow where something is revealed. The poem achieves a beautiful relationship between the revelatory dream and near and physical reality. There is an ultimate integration:

> *i have gone to the root cellar*
> *for potatoes, winter potatoes*
> *to boil a pot of tubers*
> *to set for a winter supper*
> *while we listen for a thaw in the wind,*
> *playing over the cherry grove*
> *soft as felted ivories.*

In these poems, which deal with relation, with life in and of a place, it is often the hands' work to dance; to make evident. The "ghosts of the hands" of mother, lover, friend, execute movement and embody story. By means of the work of the hands we see in these poems a sense of orthodoxy of experience. There is a path of touch, of sense, by which a profile, a fruit, or those "performers", autumn leaves, unlock meaning. In the poem "washing garden greens on an evening in mid-june", a meditative song of friendship, Candyce writes:

the tiny blue waves of your round hand
roll toward me
breaking gently against the shores
of my kitchen. gently churning
the sands. my sails
caught full, pulled by the moon
of your words.

In these poems, so richly autobiographical, sensual, and tender, we feel the determination to make a strong and well-charted journey; to make of one's own life, the dance; that which brings itself into relief, and freefalls into the near and familiar life beyond the poem's rim.

Jenné Andrews

it's all you know
for nights and nights
like burning pines
brilliant, flashing, done and gone.

past the window, through the white
his gills glint gold and green,
hurt your eyes. you dream
you're sure
but sheets turn slippery
you've lost count
of months of moods
just for seeing, just for smelling,
just to move the night.

then in he comes with pioneer grin,
it's spring, the snow
is water, brown the river moves
the ground swells green.
and who can't dance now
who can't see
straightclear through clouds
the edge of sky
where worlds touch worlds
and what don't die
starts over.

downstream quick
the current sweeps you
swift silt ride through lilyglen
pool of rainbow for my bed.
a fish's truckstop, flashing fins,
passage onto wilder shores.

and when the day
fills all its corners
we walk out
our shoulders rubbing,
you look this way,
i look that while water
wraps us anyway
and my moon's in your sun
for good.
yet you drift past
whistling lowly.
thought i'd seen you
thought i'd held your shimmer balanced.
spreading color, spending free
the time it takes
to search the fish haunts,
stalking pisces in moonchild's sea.

harbor

three old men sit
in the harbor.
they know all the boats,
the schedules
the hour each day the ferry
leaves for oslo.
sit in their shirtsleeves
faces puffed red
from the scorch off saltwater
off the white hulls.
they tell harbor stories
wipe their mouths of beer
and sweat.

sun sets red across the water.
they hold it on the horizon
with heavy eyes,
and when convinced
of the coming night
move slowly
with the world
back to dark rooms
where one must turn on
one's own light.

at the barre
for renee vosevitch

the tchaikovsky still played
but our exercise at the barre
was ended.
this we knew.
at first we collapsed, hung our arms
over the barre
breathing hard.
the tchaikovsky continued.
the old man stood in a haze over you
and your head was bent,
your hands on your hips.
he was talking and we could not hear
but you nodded.
his face was the face
of a madman who has seen
paradise
and you nodded.

we held our breath now.
our heavy thigh muscles,
our strong bodies
loose like wet fur and heavy.
he stood over you and spoke
softly, his words beat
and beat through your haze.
like strange birds they caught
in the dark of your face
and grew brilliant.
in silence we stared, our damp tights
stuck to our legs, the left-over legs
that would not matter to the world.

our stares could not penetrate the corner
where you stood in secret ceremony
while tchaikovsky played on
into the dry january night.
and we stood, as in a mime ballet, a study
in pink and black
wondering at the magic in the old man's voice
in his wet eyes
and in your child's head
bent to this music.

II

the dance

the components of grace slowly come into relief

washing garden greens on an evening in mid-june

for kris skoog wohnsen

1.

the leaves curl in my fingers
under the cold tap water.
radishes, lettuce, and mint
my kitchen fragrant with
the washing.
the smell of sun rises
above the sink, above the
green origami design floating
about my wrists.
here in the dusk i think of you
walking to your garden on the farm
the sun there in wisconsin high
over the dairy pastures
over the ribbon knolls
stringing beads of towns.
their indian names roll off
children's tongues like the sweet
cream and cheese in their
grandparent's barn.
you, down the leafy rows that sun caught
the ruby pierced through your left ear
the ear listening
just above the heart
the ear curling pale and close
to the head
under the dark swaying hair.
you mark rows of pumpkin
and corn.

dusk has gathered its yarns of light
into a single-color ball.
as it fails, evening takes on the alley.

2.

no outward sign given.
the fur smooth, no leak
of life apparent. but then
it was dark.
headlights beamed past,
bursts of stale light
reviewed the animal form.
he lifted the dead weight
into my trunk. i could not.
the thought of the cold fur
the heavy stilled blood underneath.
suddenly, all the bones in my arms
broken.

an orange tom slinks down
the violet wash alley.
red taillights swerve to avoid him.
rubies swaying in the dark.

3.

your letter open on the kitchen table.
the tiny blue waves of your round hand
roll toward me
breaking gently against the shores
of my kitchen. gently churning
the sands. my sails
caught full, pulled by the moon
of your words.
talk of the farm. summer living. no mention
of your husband, though your fingers, writing,
catch light on the half-moon nails
his nails and yours, identical.

here in the night kitchen my child
has joined me. he reaches through the greens
to the glow at the bottom of the still,
dark water.
now they sway, the radishes,
like so many scattered jewels.

the plain therapy of new england

high up the timberline
north of quebec
rains gather
and the sky here, over vermont
is black with no bottom to it.
night has transformed the gentle hills
into something terrible,
has sprung faces on the elements,
called them gods.

the dark is a shelter.
a strong-smelling canopy
over this outrageous night
as the shelter of animal skin,
the spirit of the animal guarding
the waiting door,
bending over the buffalo prairie
the fury prairie, quick with wildflowers.
no widow's walks.

here, untended dark
fleshes out the fear which
prevents one, now,
from stepping off the back porch
to part the pitch, kitchen light
shining at the shoulders,
face absorbed into light's
thirsty absence.
a fear which sends us back
inside
to sit in lamplight.
or seek out a friend in an
upstairs room.

and, catching one's own image in the
hall's blank window,
to be assured we are no less
in the dark
and to wait out his void
with the patience of the land
and in the quiet shelter of everything else
that cannot be controlled.

the alliance of new sisters
for jeanie walker

february.
she stood at the open door
watching the sky dip
its grey edges
to the scarred winter fields.
the land as it fell away
past the wooden porch railing
past the farthest hills
stared cold into the sky face
slashed black by wax wings
of suspended crows.
she felt old as the season was,
old and dry.
her eyes hurt
from the seeing.

in another room
another woman shut her eyes
skin stretched clean as cream
over forearms moving white
into darting hands.
hands falling like snow
over ivory keys.
snow circling like crow
above thistle.

pause of music.
pause of hands' snowfall
upon ivory.
the somber woman at the door
steps back from the cold air,
her hand poised at her hair
her hair smelling of wind
now,
and the rusty screen door.

naming the parts we keep
for pierre delattre

this is for the part of you
that came to be saved
in my winter kitchen
when the house was out of oil
and i sat by the oven in my boots
listening to aretha franklin
reading franklin brainerd's poems
about the missouri.
your son had left that night
returned to california taking with him
your family
your dead wife
the way you left her
the way you found her
the way you found me, burgundy blessed
in that cold kitchen chair
listening to your fear of stumbling
across love in the dark
of your heart
and i held you all night like the child
we were trying for.

this is for the part of you
that stayed public.
all those meals at different tables
all those performances,
leading up to that morning,
you, naked by the icicle window,
in the distance the frozen lake
pale yellow with winter sun.
on the windowsill a geranium
blooming as if life went on as usual.

the day your son left, with his clear
angel voice and your bright hair
he sat alone in the dim sunroom, rocking
as dusk came on, and faded
into the frosted air like rosewood smoke,
the last breath of a vivaldi trill.
the day your son left i washed out
hung up and rebraided this part of you
like a frayed rug, too worn,
too well used to seem otherwise
so sorely needed in the chilly room
but not suitable.
and you, lost in ritual, readying
for your sunday lover, told me,
in your busyness,
of the many comings, the constant
epiphanies. my litany, leaving
your kitchen table
sought the spirit to enter
sought end to that midwest prairie winter.

but there is only this part of you.
this outline.
gifts reclaimed under the new moon,
a harvest unshared.
perhaps there was no planting this year.
perhaps the seeds all blew away.

so to that other part of you
which never stood full in the circle
of firelight
perhaps that part shall come to dinner
some spring evening.
let's say in june
let's say to split the solstice
to save something more sacred
than ourselves.

let's say to save a winter geranium
blooming at the center of a tablefull of guests
and at the head
somebody's graceful-armed grandmother
head tilted back
flinging her blessings
like golden planting seeds
joyfully
into the moist wind.

letter from denmark
for laurie potter

the rain falls outside
your early morning kitchen.
your husband still asleep
your best friend in the guest room
you sit alone among your pottery,
a young farm wife
old hands in her lap
mysteries
between the lines of the palm.
on the table in front of you
the opened letter.
the thin envelope blends into the
smear of grey beyond the window sill
its foreign stamp a tiny flame
licking through the morning mail
a square of heat in your fingers.

women reach for women
and turn to men.
you shall sit like this for years
in your pasture kitchen
the early rain in the yard.
as i shall sit, also alone,
between us a salty web of yearning
the taste of the small hours
when the body quivers with the tissue
of light and dawn.

the ballet

days before opening night
you practised combing your hair
into a russian peasant style.
sitting on the dormitory bed
i toyed with a toe shoe
darned tight and perfect
by your mother's hand.
you were serious
and the bones in your face strong
as you pulled back the blond braids,
confiding you'd just slept
with your first man.

opening night
i put a rose
in your half of the room.

he was a revolutionary
from south america.
you finished your stage make-up
and turned, saying
he needed you there.
years later
a male from milwaukee had you
buying his bed and beer
while the satin toe shoes yellowed
at the back of the closet.

and i hear from someone
who frequents a certain bar
in l.a.
that the bones in your face
have gone soft.

piano lessons

i used to sit at piano lessons
and cry
or hear my sisters crying
in the other room.
the old woman would snap
and say tight-lipped
*'you are no good. what is wrong
with you.'*
but every year she would invite us
to her dogs' birthday party.
only the dogs got hats.
in summer
her funny smell would fill
the screen porch
where we waited our turns
to be defeated.
i would sit in the hammock
with the green terry cover,
and the candy
in those crystal dishes
(we never really knew if it
was there to eat)
it always tasted a million years old.

the emperor's new teeth

from the beginning
i could not sleep on my stomach
my breasts mounding up
while in your secret time you
gathered yourself.
the heart first—in just two weeks.
then the brain.
and then some ornery persistence
that kicked like a sousa brass parade
all day at the office
all night (propped now
on exactly five foam pillows)
bringing us here, to this day,
a march snowstorm,
the night a battlefield for you
as tooth enemies blast your mouth.
you scream and grip me
and later, hours later
when i think we've both lost all vision
you succumb to sleep,
take her smooth lead.
i counter the coffee
with a water glass of beaujolais
to join you, my dreamer
in gathering up the seams
of the night.

putting up against winter

it's july
and everything's sweet.
all through rural minnesota
folks sing of healthy crops,
soybeans so thick
goodhue county alone
could feed half of china.
every stretch of dirt
from waseca to st. peter
is buttoned with roadside braggarts hawking
foot-long ears of sugarbite corn
ripe tomatoes bursting their sacks
smooth honeydew
and berries.
a vernal thanksgiving
piled into tall paper bags
lined up like brown sunday children
in a row
across the backseat of the car.

july. too hot to make love
you say. you don't say
much.
you take her letters to the bathroom
lock the door.
later in the month you pack
and head west.
it's my birthday
but you're in love with oregon
and all that.

it's my time.
i've even got a full moon
cooking up the sky
healing the planter's sagging back,
plumping the harvest.
you congratulate me, long distance,
on my reaping. i'm putting up the bounty
against northern blizzards.
i know what stranded is
and stock the pantry.
eating garden pickles in january
could save some of us.

still
i'd rather be her.
rather be stupid about tilling
and tractors and home preserving.
rather just lie back
against that pacific ocean landscape
while you ripen in me.

waitress poem
for charlie title

a waitress cannot afford affairs
with men in the arts.
men with long dry fingers
and dewy eyes.
men who cry into their mashed potatoes
in a full dining room
thinking of musetta's waltz.
who don't touch their potatoes
at all, but stare
into the red eyes of the
empty wine glass
tug at their ill-fitting evening suits
and sweat.
and never have correct change.

a waitress cannot be expected
to take long weekends by the shore
with men in the arts.
men who believe there is mercy
in the marrow of wave
who wander by tide-covered banks
in a moonfever, alone,
returning at dawn to the cabin bed.
a waitress cannot lie awake there
in wait amid antiseptic guest linen
cannot anticipate the
salt water moods of such
fine boned men
who'd just as soon lay down
with a library
as with a lusty woman. no

a waitress cannot afford
to become too fond of a man
who dreams with his eyes wide open
his tongue lodged in his heart.
and so
this is not a poem to you.
this is a weekly waitress report
to say vegetables matter
and precise tipping matters
and there is no sense to
an overdone waltz.

but jesus one time the waitress
got a bit of a scare
seeing your eyes in the polished silver
your tears in the crystal
your quivering hand like the violinist's solo
at the lovers' table
red roses like fire, like fretting
blue hearts.

but she took the night off,
staying away from restaurants
reading the newspaper,
and the next day
refused to wait on any man
arriving with music
scrolled on his cuffs.

passage

there was a crossing of waters.
from the island
where your children climbed rocks
hurling plum pits, calling out
pirates' names
to the shores of the june lake,
and their mother
talking melville and little league
with other mothers of other boys,
the sun burning through her hair
as she leaned back
to watch us leave.

the boat sped like a
water rocket,
the engine putting up such a
sound barrier, it could have been
perfectly still.
it could have been a street
in st. louis, a winter night
and we could have been those
southern lovers, again
waking in the mornings
with a freighttrain for a mind.
sucking the air from
each other's mouths,
having teaparties on the ceiling
buoyed up by the messages
at the bottom of each cup.

the boat sped like a
water rocket
and there were no words.
i stared at you through dark glasses.
you pointed to a catamaran.
the waves shifted.
for a moment our legs touched.
it wasn't a catamaran.
it was a february night in st. louis,
i'm sure.
because as i stared at you
through the dark glasses
snow began to fall on your face.

famine of woman

you part your bread
with a crooked strong knife
lay the pieces heavy and brown
on cold plates round the table.
each chair filled with a child
each child reaching with tiny bird eyes
afraid to reach, though
with the spindly fingers
of hungry children.
fingers can be broken
from too much hunger, from
too much reaching.

the woman who baked the bread
is red in the face
from bending at the stove.
red with the same blood that
stuck down the insides of her legs
for each child
whether or not it lived
whether or not it sits now
still and polite
or was sent from supper.
the woman who baked the bread
keeps a knife stronger
than your crooked knife
in a place no reaching can get at
but you don't know.
the plates are neither cold
nor empty to you.

they are not even plates but
dull glassy faces that stare
and stare if one dares
reach too soon or eager,
well the knife has a strong grip.
its handle was made for pounding
where a man's fist won't do.

nightwatch

the place is dark.
i pass through it
through the rooms
to our room.
my feet, bare,
know the boards, the cracks.
i shift, mothlike
through the gloom
to where you breathe slowly.
the entire room is good
with your smell.
this warms me
as no sun does.

song for the womb fruit
to croix, in utero

your father is water
through my hands
water on my heart.
and you my child
you are the ocean
and i am the tiny sea horse
passing through you.

candyce clayton was born July 13, 1949 in Madison, Wisconsin. She graduated from Macalaster College in 1971, where she taught poetry-with-dance workshops with the Macalaster Dance Co-op. Since then she has travelled in Spain and Denmark, been a writer-in-residence at a Minnesota state hospital, and participated in the Poetry Outloud Tour. Several of her poems have been anthologized in *Zero Makes Me Hungry* (Scott, Foresman, & Co., 1976) and in the children's anthology *A Porcupine Book of Verse* (Concordia Publishing, 1974). Candyce now lives in St. Paul with her son, Croix Cambria Clayton, where she continues to study ballet and works with the Minnesota Poets in the Schools Program.

HOLY COW! Press is a new Midwestern publisher featuri[ng]
new work by both young and well-known writers. The fi[rst]
books are:

at the barre by candyce clayton
letters to tomasito by Thomas McGrath
BROTHER SONGS—an anthology of male writing

HOLY COW! Press books are edited and designed by J[im]
Perlman. This book was typeset at the West Coast Print Cen[ter]
(Berkeley, California) where 750 copies were printed Fall, 19[77].
Thanks to John McBride for patience and help.

1-6-90

PS 3553
L3.87
A9

Clayton, Candyce, 1949-

At the barre: poems.

NORMANDALE COMMUNITY COLLEGE
9700 FRANCE AVENUE S.
BLOOMINGTON, MN 55431